Masters of Loyalty

*How to turn your sales force
into a loyalty force.*

DUANE SPARKS

The Sales Board, Inc.

Copyright © 2006 by Duane Sparks

Masters of Loyalty is available at special discounts when purchased
in bulk for premiums and sales promotions as well as for fund-rais-
ing or educational use. Special editions or book excerpts can also be
created to specification. For details, contact The Sales Board at the
address below.

The Sales Board, Inc.
15200 25th Ave. N.
Minneapolis, MN 55447
(800) 232-3485
www.TheSalesBoard.com

ISBN: 0-9753569-9-2

Printed in the United States of America

First Printing October 2006

FORWARD

"Masters of Loyalty" is a wonderful description of who we want to become at my company, PrintingForLess.com. This book is a magnificent guide for getting there.

You will find an interesting dynamic between the "what" and the "how." The business world is immersed in fog and nonsense about what "customer loyalty" means. The story Duane Sparks tells in these pages cuts through that fog brilliantly by demonstrating that genuine loyalty is a relationship formed between people, not corporate entities. He describes exactly what loyalty looks like and feels like, and where it comes from. His portrayal of loyal customer relationships, and why they arise, rings true and accurate. It would be true regardless of the particular methods he recommends for building those relationships. If you, yourself, have ever been genuinely loyal to a supplier, you will see what I mean.

But the great utility of this book is that it *does* describe a systematic, step-by-step way to forge genuinely loyal, long-lasting relationships with clients—not just how to sell products and services, but how to sell loyalty.

I have been a believer in *Action Selling* since I learned the system 10 years ago while with another company. We have used its principles to build PrintingForLess.com into the largest e-commerce commercial printer in the United States. *Action Selling* has become the operating system for every relationship we have. It connects our employees, customers, business partners, and suppliers. But as we realized when we read this book, we still haven't "mastered" the system.

Our model salesperson is a customer-oriented technical expert who has been taught how to sell. Since *Action Selling* is a process, technical people tend to "get" the selling part. Customers love working with them because they get their questions answered. And our salespeople love working for us because the system makes them successful.

That's something else Sparks is right about: Salespeople can't sell loyalty to customers unless they, themselves, feel loyalty for their own company.

Now that we know what a high-quality business relationship is supposed to look like, we constantly evaluate our own vendors on how well they build loyalty. Unfortunately, many of them demonstrate "how NOT to." Our employees now recognize exactly why that is.

Thanks to *Action Selling*, our people already knew how to sell in a way that tends to build loyalty. Thanks to this book, they now know explicitly that loyalty itself is *always* the most important thing they're selling. And they know the precise steps to becoming Masters of Loyalty.

Andrew S. Field
President/CEO
PrintingForLess.com
America's Print Shop

Introduction

How we get 'customer loyalty' wrong.

L ike any business owner, I shop among various vendors for most of the goods and services my company needs. Salespeople who can offer higher quality, better service, or a lower price often find me a willing listener—at least until they, themselves, do too little listening and too much talking.

But in one area where my company relies on outside help, I am loyal to a particular supplier. By "loyal" I don't just mean that I'm satisfied with this vendor or that I have no complaints. I mean that I have *stopped shopping*. I can't imagine an offer from one of this supplier's competitors that would tempt me away. The relationship that I enjoy with the firm is too valuable, to me and to my company, for me to consider giving it up.

This vendor does good work at competitive prices—that's a given. But I'm sure that, if I cared to look, I could find a lower price. I could probably find quality and services that looked as good, too, at least on paper. I don't care. It's the relationship that has had me stuck like glue for 15 years and counting.

Now, here's a point that gets missed in almost all discussions about things that companies can do to build loyal, lasting relationships with their customers: As with every truly powerful relationship that you or I have ever had, this one is not actually with a corporate entity. It's with a person. Specifically, a salesperson. His company just reaps the benefits.

My guy won a small piece of my business in his specialty area 15 years ago. Soon he had all of it. He is deep into my company with his relationships; he knows all of my key people, regardless of their positions on the organization chart. He knows my wife, my children, my best friends—and I know his. He knows my business as well as any employee I have. We have solved a lot of problems together.

If I create a new product, he is involved in the strategy as well as in the design and execution. I have learned that I avoid a thousand headaches if I rely on him not just as a supplier but as a business partner. He is as complete a "solution" as I could wish.

His name is Kevin Mergens. His business happens to be printing. In addition to being his own best salesperson, Kevin is the owner of Absolute Print Graphics in Minneapolis. His company printed this book. He helped to edit it, too, though that role isn't in his job description. If he learned to write books, I wouldn't even need me.

Satisfaction vs. Loyalty

When companies say they want more loyal customers, they mean they want customers who give the company a greater share of their business over a longer period of time. Organizations spend a great deal of time and energy on efforts to persuade customers to become loyal.

Those efforts often take the form of loyalty programs that provide incentives for repeat business. Examples in the business-to-consumer world include airline frequent-flyer programs and the discount cards offered by retailers such as booksellers, grocery stores, and pet-supply outlets.

In the business-to-business (B2B) world, loyalty programs aim to encourage large-volume or long-term buying by offering bulk discounts and/or special packages of services or technology for major (or at least steady) clients. In any case, the point of loyalty programs is to make the sponsoring company the customer's supplier of first choice.

Here's the trouble with loyalty programs: Like most products and services today, they have become commodities, easily copied by competitors. Launch a brilliant new loyalty program that begins taking business away from your competitors, and they will match it in a matter of months—if not weeks or days.

Customers will be attracted to your loyalty program, and satisfied by it, only until they are wooed away by another program. And, loyalty program or no, you are their "supplier of first choice" only until the next choice appears. Try opening a trendy new restaurant that will remain trendy for longer than a year or two.

Products, services, programs, policies, and procedures—things your *company* does in the name of building loyalty—can be important. But even the best company-level initiatives create only satisfaction, not real loyalty. They leave you vulnerable to competitors.

"Satisfaction" won't cut it. True loyalty does not exist until a customer has *stopped shopping*, as I have for my printing needs, and is *highly resistant to your competitors' appeals*. Unless you are Harley-Davidson, and your customers tattoo your corporate logo on their bodies, your products or your brand won't generate that kind of loyalty. Neither will your programs or other corporate-level initiatives. This is especially true in the B2B world, where rewards programs do practically nothing to keep customers from leaving.

What's wrong with customers who are merely satisfied? Just this, as research shows:

> • 75% of customers who leave a company for a competitor say they were satisfied or even "very satisfied" with the company they left.
>
> • Only 25% of customers who defect from a company say they left for a lower price—but 50% of salespeople *think* that's why their customers defect.
>
> • Only 10% of customers leave because their needs have changed. Salespeople think a full third of their clients leave for that reason.
>
> • *75% of customers actually leave a supplier because of the lack of a solid sales relationship.* But only 20% tell the salesperson that this is why they're leaving.

Source: The Sales Board, Inc.

From sales force to loyalty force

That last statistic suggests why loyalty programs appeal to the wrong causes of customer defections. It also suggests where the answer really lies for companies that want customers who are loyal in the most valuable sense of the word—customers who have stopped shopping and are deaf to competitors' appeals. When it comes to generating real loyalty, a company's greatest asset is the potential of its sales force.

People won't go deaf to a company's competitors. They will go deaf to the competitors of another person. Think about it. Have you ever felt so loyal to a supplier that you stopped shopping? If so, what made you feel that way? Was it really the company? Or was it a person?

Any customers, but especially B2B clients, are most apt to become loyal when they have developed a bond with a particular kind of salesperson. This kind of salesperson acts as a consultant, an orchestrator of resources and, above all, a relationship builder.

Salespeople who are skilled at generating loyalty understand that loyalty itself must be earned and sold. Those in B2B situations market not just their companies and their products but *themselves* to the client's entire enterprise. They don't fall into the trap of thinking that the ultimate decision maker (the person with budget authority) is the only buyer who counts and that the rest of those folks—product users, technical specialists, other influencers—are merely obstacles in their path as they rush to gain the decision maker's ear.

A company with 100 Kevin Mergens in it would rule the world. But he is a rarity. Why? Because the vast majority of salespeople don't act as loyalty generators. They don't understand that the underlying purpose of every client call should be to *sell loyalty* by strengthening their personal relationship with the client. And even if that idea makes sense to them, they don't know how to do it.

That's why I wrote this book.

*Even during a "successful" sales call, the needle is
always moving one way or the other.*

Masters of Loyalty

Most salespeople define a successful call as one in which the customer is satisfied with the dialogue or the presentation, and therefore
buys something—or at least agrees to take some positive action.
Suppose they raised their sights and their definition of success?

The Loyalty Generator diagram represents a gauge of the direction in which the salesperson's *relationship* with the customer is
moving during the course of every sales call. It applies even to "successful" calls, because if the customer isn't at least satisfied, the call
fails.

To the degree that the needle moves toward "loyal," the concept of a successful sales call takes on new and greater meaning. The customer is not only buying but becoming immunized against the salesperson's competitors. The customer is deciding to stop shopping.

I said above that most salespeople don't understand that the underlying purpose of every call should be to sell loyalty. This applies even to many of those who have been trained in *Action Selling*, which I believe is the best system yet devised for selling not just products or services, but loyalty. (Yes, I'm biased.)

The numbered gears in the Loyalty Generator diagram represent the nine Acts of *Action Selling*. Their size represents their relative importance in selling loyalty. A genuinely loyal customer is the goal. *Action Selling* is the manual that tells you how to achieve that goal.

Some salespeople grasp intuitively that *Action Selling* is not only a sales system but a loyalty-generation system. They become black-belts, operating at a master's level. Others don't quite get it. Their sales performance may improve dramatically, but they do not reach their full potential as loyalty generators. And their companies don't reap the full benefits of that potential.

In my previous books, I have described the *Action Selling* system, how it works to lift the game beyond the trap of price competition, and why questioning skills are so vital to success. In this book, I have attempted to describe what selling looks and feels like at the black-belt level...the master's level...the loyalty-generation level.

In a master's-level sales call, you can actually see loyalty happen. Capturing that look and feel was my major goal. *Action Selling* itself is explained only to the extent necessary to show how loyalty can be built in a systematic, replicable way.

You also will find a sub-theme that is especially important to sales managers and executives. Loyalty is multidimensional. Salespeople are much better at *selling* loyalty to customers when they *feel* loyalty to their own companies.

Like my previous books, this one tells a story. It's a story about Mike, a marketing vice president who has a problem your organization just might share, and Tony, a salesperson who has the solution. The complication: Because Tony is a master, he can't understand why others have the problem. That makes it tough for him to communicate the answer.

Does Tony succeed in getting the message across? That's for you to decide. For your sake, and your company's, I hope so.

Here's to *real* customer loyalty. Good Action Selling!

Duane Sparks
Chairman, The Sales Board
Author of Action Selling

CONTENTS

PREFACE

There's something strange about this loyalty thing.

By the time the plane reached cruising altitude, dawn had broken. The passenger in seat 2-A turned his attention from the window and asked the flight attendant in the first-class cabin for another cup of coffee. His clothing had already pegged him as a business traveler, but now something in his manner caused the attendant to update her appraisal. *Another worried executive*, she thought. *Like so many these days. Is it just me, or did the guys in good suits used to look a lot happier?*

Her perception was accurate. Mike was, indeed, an executive—a vice-president of marketing, to be exact—and he certainly was worried. But the flight attendant could not have guessed just how peculiar this particular business trip was.

Mike himself could scarcely believe the reason he was on the plane to Phoenix. *My job depends on some mysterious sales rep I've never met,* he thought. *Tony, my man, whoever you are, I hope you can show me a way out of this mess. Because I sure can't figure out the answer.*

The flight attendant was right about another thing. Mike used to be a lot happier. Only a year ago, he was a corporate hero. It was at his urging that his company trained and certified its sales force in a new system called *Action Selling*. At the time, the company's annual rate of sales growth was stuck at 2.5 percent, average for its mature industry. After the training, the growth rate more than doubled to 5.1 percent. The new system was a tremendous hit with the sales force, and Mike's CEO was delighted with the results. At least for a while.

But the CEO wanted more. He was under pressure from stockholders to increase both revenue and profits at a faster clip. When the quarterly numbers came in 90 days after the training was completed and showed that the new sales system was a smashing success, there had been jubilation. But a month later, the CEO called Mike into his office.

"We still need more customers, and we need more business from current customers," he said. "I suppose it doesn't exactly surprise you that those two things are at the top of my list," he added with a smile.

Not exactly, Mike thought. *You're a CEO, after all.*

"Let me explain," the chief executive continued. "Analysts no longer evaluate companies in our industry purely on sales growth. They want to see us grow our base of customers as well as the revenue from our base. The sales growth that we have accomplished with *Action Selling* needs to continue, but specifically with our current customers. If we want our stock price to rise, we have to do it with what's called 'organic sales growth.' That means we need more business from the customers we've already got."

I couldn't ask for a better opening than this, Mike thought. *Am I a proactive marketing VP or what? Get ready, Boss, because here comes Mike's Greatest Hits-Volume 2.*

"You're reading my mind," he said. "I've been thinking the same thing. And I believe the solution to organic growth lies in customer

> ## 'The solution to organic growth lies in customer loyalty.'

loyalty. We need to elevate our sales and service goal from 'satisfied' customers and start creating more genuinely loyal ones. We need to bind them to us somehow so that we get more of their business, more consistently and over a longer term."

Mike noticed the CEO's eyes brighten.

Eagerly, he began to outline the new program he had been planning. Pulling out a document he had brought to the meeting, Mike pointed to research showing that 40 percent of "satisfied" customers will leave a company for a competitor without hesitation. And 75 percent of customers who switch suppliers do so despite being "satisfied" or "very satisfied" with the original one.

"Our customer-satisfaction surveys have been measuring the wrong thing," Mike said. "We have to turn satisfied customers into loyal customers." The way to do that, he argued, was with a loyalty program. In the same way that airlines use frequent-flyer programs and retail stores offer discount cards, he said, "we should offer customers a special incentive to give more of their business to us and less to the competition."

Mike's proposal was a loyalty program he called TechShare. To high-volume customers, TechShare would offer elite status for pricing and delivery, automated ordering with instant access to supply chain inventories, online access to training and technical help, and more. The program wouldn't require adding any expensive new capabilities. It was essentially a new way to package services that the company already could provide.

"The *Action Selling* system doubled our rate of growth," he concluded, a not-so-subtle reminder of his recent victory. "I think if we give the reps TechShare to sell, we can double our rate again."

The CEO was sold. Six months ago, TechShare had launched—with $2 million worth of advertising and marketing support. The program was Mike's baby, his pride and joy.

And it bombed. In the wake of TechShare's launch, the growth rate barely budged. After six months, the average sales rep, company-wide, had sold the TechShare program to exactly three clients. (*Three?* Mike thought, the incredulity rising yet again. *Three?*) Most reps had signed up only one or two accounts. A number of them had sold none at all.

Needless to say, the CEO wasn't interested in sharing blame for the decision to run with the program. "This is your $2 million dog," he told Mike. "Cure it or shoot it."

Reports from the field indicated that customers saw nothing specifically wrong with TechShare. But competitive suppliers offered loyalty programs, too, and customers couldn't see much difference between them. Like the products Mike's company sold, special incentive programs had become commodities. The *Action Selling* system had helped the sales reps tremendously when it came to differentiating their products. But they seemed at a loss when the "product" was TechShare.

There were exceptions, of course. *And in the entire company*, Mike thought, his mind skipping to his present mission, *the biggest, most glaring exception is you, Tony.*

For the past year, the Phoenix office had been the company's star operation, reporting the highest revenue

> ## 'Like products, special incentive programs have become commodities.'

and the best margins. Phoenix also had sold twice as many TechShare programs as the second-best branch. Why? How? When Mike called the branch manager to investigate, the answer was simple enough. But it only raised more questions.

"It's Tony," the manager said. "I have five sales reps, but he's the reason we're outstanding. Without him, we'd be about average. I wish I could clone him."

While each of the other four salespeople had signed up three TechShare accounts, Tony so far had sold 30. But it wasn't just TechShare, the manager explained. "Tony gets more business and better margins out of almost all his accounts, regardless of whether they sign up for the loyalty program."

Why? "I wish I knew," the manager said. "His customers just seem to love him."

Tony was some kind of born superstar salesperson then?

Not at all, the manager said. "That's the strange thing. He's been with us four years, and until he got the *Action Selling* training he was average. It's just in this past year that he caught fire."

As Mike knew, the manager pointed out, since the new system

was introduced, the average rep's sales performance had improved significantly. "But Tony's performance skyrocketed. He gives all the credit to *Action Selling*. But why does he seem to get more out of it than the others? Like I said, if I knew that, I'd clone him."

And if I knew, and I could clone him, Mike thought, *maybe I could rescue my job before it's too late*. For the first time in months, he saw a ray of hope…by the name of Tony.

With the branch manager's OK, Mike had called Tony. He explained that he was doing some research into how TechShare could be sold more effectively. "You've outsold our average reps 10 to one," he said. "What are you doing that the others aren't?"

As the manager had warned, however, Tony seemed genuinely at a loss. "I just use the *Action Selling* system," he said. "Hey, it has helped every rep in the company."

Yes, but why was the boost in Tony's performance so exceptional? Tony had no idea. Mike probed, but got nowhere. In some way, Mike began to suspect, Tony must understand the system on a deeper level than most. If he couldn't explain how or why, maybe it was for the same reason a fish couldn't describe water. *Is it something so obvious to him that he can't imagine the rest of us don't know it?* Mike thought. *I need to see this guy work.*

Mike asked if he could come to Phoenix and shadow Tony for a day—accompany him on some sales calls as an observer. Tony was happy to oblige. "Are you kidding?" he said. "My clients would be happy to meet one of our executives. You'd be helping me with Act 5."

Act 5 was *Action Selling* terminology for a step in the sales process called "Sell the Company." *Well, he sure thinks in the system's terms*, Mike thought.

His reverie was broken by the pilot's announcement that the plane was on final approach to Phoenix.

I'm counting on you to have the answer I need, Tony, even if you don't know what it is, Mike thought. *If I can figure out what you're doing differently, maybe I can replicate it. And if I can do that, I can save TechShare—and my job. One more remark about $2 million dogs, and I'd better sharpen up my resume.*

As the plane touched down, Mike turned his gaze back to the window with a mixture of hope and desperation. At least it was better than the pure desperation he had felt for months.

Chapter 1

THE BLACK BELT IN LOYALTY

Mike gets a glimpse—but a glimpse of what?

"So would you like to go ahead and make us your primary supplier?" Tony asked.

"Yes, I would," Janice answered. "Let's get started."

"Thanks, Janice," Tony said. "I appreciate your business. I promise we're going to make you very happy with this decision. Now, when shall we schedule a quick training session for your staff on how the ordering system will work? Would Friday be convenient?"

"Let me check the calendar. Yes, let's say Friday at 9 a.m." Janice turned to Mike. "You'd better hang onto this guy," she said, nodding toward Tony.

No kidding, Mike thought. He managed to smile back at her as he struggled to sort out his thoughts.

Mike was in awe, that much he knew. But he wasn't sure *why*.

On the surface, everything he had seen and heard during the morning's sales call was perfectly familiar. Tony had followed the steps of the *Action Selling* system, just as it was taught.

In previous meetings with Janice he obviously had identified and gained agreement on her key needs. His concise presentation of the primary-supplier arrangement had been targeted straight at those needs, hitting all of the client's hot buttons, with no extraneous talk about features or benefits that didn't concern her. He had asked for her commitment and received it. Mike even recognized the follow-up business about the training appointment as a textbook example of what *Action Selling* called Act 8: *After the sale, schedule a "future event" to get the buyer looking forward to the next step instead of backward to the investment she just made.*

To anyone who knew the system, everything that happened during the call was as plain as day. Yet Mike felt as if he had watched the transaction unfold at some new, higher level.

He had a handle on one big difference, at least. *Tony asks for commitment*, Mike thought, *but he asks for bigger commitments than our other reps.*

The first clue to that one had come early, shortly after Tony picked up Mike at the airport and they got acquainted. They would make three calls today, Tony explained. The first was on Janice, who had been a customer for about six months. Starting from a trial basis, he had slowly gained a greater percentage of her business.

"She now does about 30 percent of her buying from us, with the rest split mainly among three of our competitors," Tony explained. "Today I'm going to present an arrangement that would make us her primary, first-call supplier. We'd get at least 90 percent of her business. My Commitment Objective is for her to agree to grant us primary-supplier status."

At the sound of "Commitment Objective," Mike noted again, as he had on the phone, that Tony seemed to think naturally in *Action Selling* terms. "So you're going to sign her up for TechShare?" he asked.

"That's part of it," Tony answered. "TechShare has features that will meet some of her needs, so I've incorporated it into the proposal."

Part of it? Mike thought, stung on behalf of his brainchild. *For a guy who has sold 30 TechShare programs, you seem awfully cavalier about it.*

When he listened to Tony presenting the primary-supplier deal to Janice, however, Mike realized that the loyalty program he had so carefully devised was, indeed, only one element in the solution Tony described. TechShare was in the proposal solely because it addressed certain key needs that Janice and Tony had identified. At least, that was how he presented it.

In explaining TechShare, Tony covered its cost-saving advantages, but he stressed it mainly as a good way to streamline the processes of returns, credits, and inventory balancing. Those were the issues, Mike observed, that really grabbed Janice's attention.

But the main reason Janice committed to Tony's larger objective—to grant his company first-call status for high-demand products—was because of commitments he made to her in return. In particular, he vowed to be relentless in finding and delivering the products she needed, when she needed them—and Janice believed him.

He has built some serious trust here, Mike noted.

Make that extreme trust, he thought, finally putting his finger on

'Tony has built some serious trust here.'

the strangest element of the sales call. Now that he thought about it, one part of the discussion had been downright remarkable.

It happened while Tony was talking about Janice's need for greater efficiency in her product-acquisition process. At one point he broke off awkwardly, as if catching himself on the verge of saying something he shouldn't.

Janice stepped right into the silence. Turning to Mike, she said: "It hasn't been announced yet, but we're about to acquire a competitor. There will be synergies in areas including procurement. In plain English, that means some of those people probably will lose their jobs. So this is strictly confidential. But that's why I need to get product-acquisition straightened out."

Turning back to Tony, she said, "Thanks for the discretion. But go ahead."

Caught up in listening to Tony's presentation, Mike hadn't fully recognized the oddness at the time. But now it registered: *She's been discussing sensitive, confidential information with an outside salesperson? These are the kinds of needs Tony uncovers? The solution he was presenting to her is for problems she isn't even supposed to talk about? Is she just careless? Or is it him?*

"Want to grab some lunch?" Tony asked as they climbed back into the car after leaving Janice's office.

"Sure." Mike pulled out a pad and scribbled some notes:

What Tony Does:

Sets goals for bigger commitments
Unusual need identification
Extreme trust
Naturally asks for commitment

"You know," Mike said, "I'm surprised Janice has told you about the acquisition her company is planning. Does she talk that freely to everybody?"

Tony looked alarmed. "I know you'll respect her confidence, Mike," he said, in a protective tone that carried a hint of *don't you dare burn my customer.* "No, Janice isn't a blabbermouth. I'm positive none of our competitors know about this. She took a risk telling me. It's just that this is a situation she needs to prepare for, and…"

"And she trusts you," Mike finished for him. "She trusts you so much that by extension, she trusted me. Don't worry, my lips are sealed. But what I want to know is, how did you develop a relationship with her that goes that deep? I mean, it's not as if you're childhood pals, right? You've only known her for, what, six months?"

Tony was puzzled by the question. "Well, that's *Action Selling,* right? I mean, that's what it's for. That's what it does. The conversations you have with customers are completely different from the conversations you used to have. It's all right there in the system. And you're the one who brought in the system. Thanks a million, by the way."

Tony paused to gather his thoughts. "I guess I don't understand your question," he said at last. "If you'd never heard of *Action Selling,* and you asked why Janice sees me as a trusted consultant instead of a garden-variety salesperson, I'd know what to tell you. I'd say, 'Well, I learned this great sales system, and it changed everything—my whole approach to selling. Heck, my whole life.' But you *do* know how *Action Selling* works. So what can I tell you?

'I earn her trust every time I call.'

"I mean, why does Janice trust me? Because I earn her trust every time I call. Why does she tell me about her pressing needs? Because I ask her what they are. Why does she assume I genuinely want to help her address those needs? Because I do. It was *Action Selling* that taught me *how* to earn her trust, and *how* to ask the best questions to uncover needs, and *how* to show her that I'm there to help, not just to sell her something. You're the guy who introduced the system to the company. You already know all this."

'I'm there to help, not just to sell her something.'

Yeah, Mike thought, *except that somehow you "get it" in a way that most of us don't.*

"I appreciate that, Tony," he said. "But the fact remains that while all of our salespeople learn the system, you've now outsold the average rep 31 to three when it comes to TechShare. And in the call I just saw, at least, you didn't even sell TechShare as the primary solution.

"What's more," Mike continued, "practically all of our reps have built stronger relationships with customers using *Action Selling*, but I can pretty much assure you that most of them don't hear confidential corporate information on sales calls."

"Hey, it's not as if that's an everyday thing for me, either," Tony protested. "Janice just happens to be in a tight spot…"

"Which she just happened to feel comfortable talking to you about," Mike interrupted. "Let me lay my cards on the table. We need organic growth. We don't just need new customers, we need to get more business from our existing ones. We need customers who aren't just satisfied with our products and services but are loyal to us over the long haul. We need to take things to the next level. We need more salespeople who can do what you just did with Janice. Yes, I could see you were using *Action Selling*. But it's as if you do it at a black-belt level.

"Look, Tony, I don't know what the secret is and, evidently, neither do you. But you either understand that selling system in a deeper way than anyone else or you execute it

'We need customers who aren't just satisfied, but are loyal.'

better. Maybe one leads to the other, beats me. But I'd like to try to figure it out. I *need* to figure it out. Are you game?"

Tony stopped for a traffic light around the corner from the

Scottsdale restaurant where they would have lunch. "You know, one thing you just said might be significant," he mused, as if thinking aloud. "I never thought of it in these terms, but…"

"What?" Mike asked.

"You said that I don't 'even' sell TechShare as a primary solution. As if that's surprising."

"Well, isn't it?" Mike asked. "We're talking about loyalty. TechShare is our loyalty program."

Tony made a turn, and pulled into the restaurant's parking lot. "Mike, I know TechShare is your baby," he said. "I don't want to overstep here."

"You're worried you'll offend me? Believe me, Tony, I've got bigger problems than having my feelings hurt. If you think something is wrong with TechShare, please say so."

'How can you talk as if customer loyalty is about a loyalty program?'

"No, there's nothing wrong with TechShare," Tony said. "It's a great tool. What confuses me is just…Well, if you know what *Action Selling* is, how can you talk as if customer loyalty is about a loyalty *program*?"

Chapter 2

WHERE LOYALTY IS BORN

Consistency turns a sales maker
into a Loyalty Generator.

They settled into a quiet booth toward the rear of the restaurant and began to peruse the lunch menu. But Tony was more concerned with Mike's ominous silence.

"Look, Mike, that came out wrong," he said. *No kidding*, he thought, kicking himself. *You're the big boss who brought* Action Selling *into the company, so I imply that you don't understand it. Maybe I can spill my soup on you, too, and then just resign.* "I didn't mean to…"

Mike waved off the apology. "No, Tony, I'm not offended." (*All right, maybe a little*, he thought.) "I'm just thinking. There's got to be an important clue in what you said: 'How can I think that loyalty is about the TechShare program?' You've sold more programs than anyone else—a lot more—but when you sell TechShare, you're not selling loyalty? What do you mean?"

I'm not sure, Tony thought, groping for words. "Well," he said finally, "I guess I mean that the TechShare program is essentially a product. It's packaged with a name and features and benefits, like any product. Loyalty is different, isn't it? I mean, customers have to be loyal *before* they'll buy a loyalty program, don't they?"

> **'Customers have to be loyal before they'll buy a loyalty program.'**

That's clear as mud, he thought. Then inspiration came. "OK, look," he said, with more confidence. "*Action Selling* is all about differentiation, right? It's a system that tells us how to be different and better, in a tangible way, from the competition, even when the competition's products—or loyalty programs—may be virtually the same as ours. *Action Selling* tells us how to show the customer that we're offering unique solutions instead of commodities. It tells us how to communicate differently, so that we stop being order-takers and start to act like consultants or business partners. What matters isn't *what* we sell but *how* we sell, right?"

"Right," Mike said, thinking: *You see it as a consultant's communication system, not just a way to make sales? I'm not sure I ever thought of it that way.*

"Well," Tony continued, "if customers see us as a unique and valuable solution, and they'd prefer to buy from us rather than someone else, that's just another way to say they're loyal to us, isn't it? I mean, TechShare is a package—a product—that has to be differ-

> **'Loyalty comes from the perception of a valuable difference in the sales relationship.'**

entiated like any other product. But loyalty doesn't come from the loyalty program. It comes from the perception of a valuable difference in the sales relationship. Doesn't it?"

Mike thought it over. As much to himself as to Tony, he said, "If you differentiate once, you make a sale. If you differentiate the sales relationship, you make a loyal customer."

"Well...yeah," Tony said. "But now I'm confused again. *Action Selling* isn't something you use once with a new customer to get an order. It's a discipline you practice consistently, on every sales call. Consistency is what turns *Action Selling* into

> *'If you differentiate once, you make a sale. If you differentiate the sales relationship, you make a loyal customer.'*

a kind of perpetual-motion machine that generates loyalty. Don't all of our reps know that?"

I wonder, Mike thought. He made a few notes:

thinks specifically about selling loyalty
Loyalty first, then the loyalty program
Action Selling: A consultant's communication system
Uses system consistently with existing clients
Consistency creates a differentiated sales relationship

The server arrived and took their orders.

Mike reached into his briefcase and fished out a laminated card illustrating the steps of the *Action Selling* system. "Do me a favor, Tony," he said. "Walk me quickly through the system as you understand it and use it. Let me try to figure out why you're 'making more loyalty' than anyone else."

"OK," Tony shrugged. "Well, as you know, the whole thing is based on a documented fact that I was never aware of. In the course of any major sale, every customer makes five key buying decisions, always in the same order."

Using a napkin, Tony drew a question mark like the one in the *Action Selling* training materials, and divided it into segments.

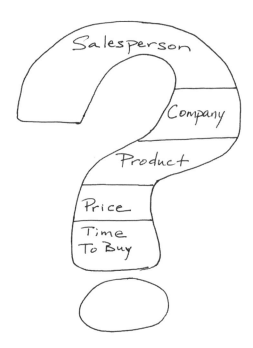

"First," he said, "the customer decides whether to 'buy' the salesperson. Then whether to 'buy' the company. Then whether the product is suitable. Then whether the price is competitive. And finally whether the time to buy is now or later.

"Whether they know it or not, customers always make those decisions in the same order," Tony continued. "That means I can't be effective at selling my product unless I have first sold myself and then sold my company. Once you understand that, the rest of the *Action Selling* system is logical and almost inevitable, don't you think?"

Yes, Mike did.

"Even if I hadn't learned the rest of the system, finding out about the five buying decisions would have helped me a lot," Tony said. "I used to think my job was to sell the product, and everything else was just sort of ancillary. Simply knowing that my first task in any sales call is always to sell myself and then to sell my company—that makes a world of difference."

Mike nodded. He had heard the same thing from other sales reps.

"One huge thing that came out of the training and hit me between the eyes is

'The salesperson who follows the Action Selling process the best wins.'

that the salesperson who follows the *Action Selling* process the best wins," Tony said. "So I stopped winging it and tried to adopt the process fully. Today I measure my performance on every sales call by how well I did at selling each of the five buying decisions.

"Obviously, that helps me troubleshoot the sales process," he continued. "If something isn't going well, I can almost always tell which decision a customer is hung up on. What hasn't the customer 'bought'? Me? The company? The product?"

Mike sat up straighter. *Do our other reps think in those terms?* He made another note:

Uses 5 Buying Decisions for sales problem solving

"So if you had trouble gaining commitment for Techshare," Mike said, "your first thought would not be, 'Why aren't they buying the loyalty program?' You'd first think, 'Have they bought me?' Then you'd think, 'Have they bought my company?' Is that right?"

"Well, sure," Tony said, as if this were perfectly obvious. "That's what it means for customers to 'buy me' or 'buy my company,' isn't it? If I'm always trying to differentiate from the competition, then

'I'm always trying to differentiate. I'm always selling loyalty.'

I'm always selling loyalty. Therefore, first they have to become loyal to me, then they have to become loyal to my company, and so on. It's just another way of saying the same thing."

Yes, it is, Mike thought. *So why haven't I seen it in that light?*

Their food arrived at the table. "Keep going," Mike said. "Take me through the system itself. I can eat and listen if you can eat and talk."

"I'll try not to do it with my mouth full," Tony said, silently adding, *you being a vice president and all.* "OK, *Action Selling* is divided into nine Acts, or nine steps in the sales process."

Act 1 takes place before the call, when the salesperson chooses a Commitment Objective, Tony explained. "This was another huge eye-opener for me," he said. "The idea is that a sales call may have several objectives, but the primary one always must be a Commitment Objective. That's a commitment you want from the customer—an agreement to take some action that will move the sales process forward.

> *Commitment Objective – an agreement to take some action that will move the sales process forward.*

"Depending on where I am in the sales process, my Commitment Objective might be for the customer to agree to buy the product—or, rather, the solution I'm proposing. Earlier in the process, it might be to get an agreement to let me meet with other decision-makers or to come back and do a more thorough needs analysis. But I *never* make a call without a Commitment Objective. No more of that nonsense where I used to just check in to see if a customer wanted to order anything."

And I already know that you set bigger, more ambitious Commitment Objectives than most of our reps, Mike thought. *The question is, how do you achieve them?* "Do Commitment Objectives relate directly to 'selling loyalty?'" he asked.

"Sure," Tony said. "For instance, if I'm calling on a current customer, it's easy to forget to have a Commitment Objective. But gaining agreement that a customer is more than just satisfied with our performance is a good loyalty Commitment Objective."

In **Act 2** the salesperson opens the call by demonstrating People Skills, Tony explained.

The salesperson begins to 'sell himself' by showing that he is personable, likeable, and above all has excellent listening skills.

> *'Loyal customers expect me to take some time for Act 2.'*

"You do this mainly by asking open-ended questions," Tony said, "questions that can't be answered with a 'yes' or 'no,' so that they encourage the customer to do most of the talking.

"Loyal customers expect me to take some time for Act 2," Tony added. "If I run into resistance here, that's a flag that loyalty may be slipping."

In **Act 3**, called Ask the Best Questions, the open-ended questions become focused more specifically on the customer's needs. Tony flipped over the laminated card on the table and pointed to the "Ask the Best Questions Map" on the back. "There's the outline of the kinds of questions I ask—about the customer, her company, the issues driving the buying decision, how the sales process will work, and so on.

"You asked why Janice trusted me enough to tell me about the acquisition," Tony said. "I don't know what to say except that in Act 2 and, especially, Act 3, I showed her that I was interested in her situation and I wanted to help in any way I could."

"But she didn't talk about the acquisition on your first call, right?" Mike asked.

"Oh, of course not," Tony said. "But obviously Act 3 keeps getting deeper the better you know the customer. I mean, Act 3 reveals different needs on your fifth call than it does on your fourth, and so on. And it gets easier to discover what *Action Selling* calls 'high-yield needs'—the real hot-button issues that make the buying decision important to the customer."

"I suppose it does if you remember to *do* an Act 3 every time you call on a client and not just in the early stages of the relationship," Mike said.

"Well, sure," Tony shrugged. "Of course. I prepare questions in advance for every sales call. Say, that might be something other reps don't do. If they don't, that could explain why I outsell them. If they're just winging it in Act 3, I think that's a huge loyalty slip."

Consistency, Mike thought again. *I know that 95 percent of salespeople don't prepare Act 3 questions before sales calls.* "Please keep going," he said.

> *'95% of salespeople don't prepare Act 3 questions before a sales call.'*

In **Act 4**, Tony continued, the salesperson and the customer Agree on Needs. "This Act is short but vital," he said. "After my questions have identified what I think are at least three key needs that really matter to the customer, I check to see if I'm right. I say, 'As I understand it, you're looking for a solution that will accomplish X, Y, and Z. Is that correct?'

"This tells me how to tailor my presentation in the next two Acts," Tony continued. "Instead of just doing a data dump that lists all the virtues of my company, and all the features and benefits of my products, I can speak directly to how my company and my products can serve specific needs that the customer has already agreed are important."

Mike nodded. "That completely changes the way you make your product presentation, doesn't it," he said.

"You bet it does," Tony agreed. "And my company presentation, too. If Act 4 is done right, you agree on differentiated needs, not commodity needs. Before I learned Action Selling, I didn't even do Act 4. There is no way to assure differentiation and loyalty without it." He took a bite of his sandwich and remembered to swallow before he spoke again.

"**Act 5** is Sell the Company," he said. "This is where I start to do a little less listening and more of the talking. Since customers won't buy my product before they have bought my company, I have to give them reasons to buy my company—not just that we're reputable and so on, but why we're a particularly good match for the customer's situation."

'It never occurred to me that my feelings about my company were especially relevant to the customer.'

Tony grinned. "Act 5 has to do with something I never appreciated before I learned *Action Selling*," he continued. "I love our company, Mike. It's a great place to work. We're innovative, we invest in our people as well as in our customers…we're really pretty extraordinary. But it never occurred to me that *my* feelings about *my* company were especially relevant to the customer."

He paused. "Actually, my 'feelings' about it probably aren't directly relevant. But I've found that when I can communicate my excitement about my company, and tie it to a need I've agreed on with the customer, that's really powerful. I like Act 5 a lot."

Mike looked at him keenly, feeling another brick drop into place. "I'll bet Act 5 is something else you do consistently, on every call, isn't it?" he asked. "I mean, not just when you're making an initial sale to a customer." *You're going to say, 'Of course,'* he thought.

"Of course," Tony said. "There's always something new going on that I can mention on any call. Like I said, we're an innovative bunch."

One reason you create loyal customers for our company, Tony, is because you're unusually loyal to it yourself, Mike thought. *Somehow we did a great job of 'selling the company' to you. I don't believe we've sold it as well to most of our reps. I'll bet most of them don't even talk about their company with current customers. Big mistake. Customers unconsciously think, "The salesperson doesn't seem loyal to this company, so why should I be loyal?"*

He made another note:

Loyalty: first sell it to our employees, THEN to customers?

"Please go on," Mike said.

"**Act 6** is 'Sell the Product,'" Tony said. "This is where I present the product or solution I want the customer to buy. In the bad old days, before *Action Selling*, this is what I thought of as the real 'selling' part. The rest of it—the conversation, the questions, the so-called need identification—was all just peripheral."

'Consistently presenting solutions to agreed upon needs earns loyalty.'

He laughed. "Now I understand that I do most of my real selling when I'm asking and listening in the earlier Acts. Act 6 is usually pretty short. I just explain what we propose to do to help with the needs that the customer and I have already agreed on. I'm a lot better than I used to be at presenting solutions to agreed-upon needs. When you do that consistently, you earn loyalty. Well, hey, you saw Act 6 with Janice this morning."

Yes, and the remarkable part was not that you're some extraordinary pitchman, Mike thought. *It was the level of the needs you had identified and could speak to. Everything you presented in Act 6 was tied so closely to a solution for her. Funny that didn't strike me earlier.*

"This is helpful, Tony," Mike said. "Take me through the rest of it."

"Okay. **Act 7** is Ask for Commitment. Whatever my Commitment

'I never waste their time. That helps loyalty grow.'

Objective is, I won't get the customer's commitment unless I come out and ask for it. I felt like an idiot during the *Action Selling* training when I realized how often I was failing to do that. Because I don't make calls without a Commitment Objective, the customer sees me as someone who gets things done. It's a productivity thing—I never waste their time. That helps loyalty grow."

"In **Act 8**," he continued, "I Confirm the Sale by thanking the customer, assuring her that she has made the right decision, and scheduling a 'future event' to get her looking forward to the next step instead of backward at the money she spent. Like with the training session for Janice."

Mike smiled, remembering. "So the training session wasn't just something that coincidentally had to be scheduled right then and there, eh?"

Tony smiled back. "Customers appreciate how professional this is. Do you think they'd rather be loyal to a pro or an amateur?"

Act 9, Replay the Call, happens after every sales call is concluded, Tony said. The salesperson mentally reviews the call, step by step, to note things that went well and things that didn't. "That way, you never stop improving your game," he said. "In the call on Janice, for instance, I should have been better prepared for the fact that you'd be in the room when the secret acquisition came up. I fumbled that part. She rescued me, but that shouldn't have been necessary."

'After every call, I ask myself, "Did my relationship get stronger or weaker?"'

"So," Mike said, "I'm thinking, 'Wow, how did he develop that level of trust with Janice?' and you're thinking, 'Wow, I need to anticipate better in unusual situations.' Is that about the size of it?"

"Well, that's what 'Replay the Call' is all about, isn't it?" Tony replied. "Oh, and one other thing might be important. After every call, I ask myself, 'Did my relationship with this client get stronger or weaker?' That's just a way of asking, 'Are they more or less loyal following this call?'"

Mike made a note:

Ties loyalty selling to every Act

Measures Loyalty gain in Act 9

"I'm sorry I can't be more help, Mike," Tony said. "I'm just parroting back the basics of *Action Selling*. The nine acts are like its skeleton. You know this stuff as well as I do. I don't have any brilliant new insights into any of it."

Your work is more brilliant than you realize, Mike thought. He waved Tony's apology aside. "No, you're doing fine. I appreciate this," he said. "You told me we'll be making two more calls today. What are our Commitment Objectives?"

Chapter 3

IT'S EXECUTION, NOT MAGIC

Masters have headaches, too.

"Our first appointment this afternoon will be a joint call with George," Tony said in response to Mike's question. "He's one of our reps here in Phoenix. George is making a TechShare call and asked me to give him some coaching before he goes in. And, of course, he wants me to help on the call. He has positioned me as some kind of TechShare expert.

"George wants to close a TechShare deal today," Tony continued. "But between you and me, George doesn't get it. He thinks that selling a loyalty program will make his customer loyal—which means he has it backwards. He also seems to think I've got some magic potion that I can sprinkle on his customer. One call on this client is not going to result in a loyal customer for George. Not even with you and me on the call."

> **'George has it backwards.'**

"So the Commitment Objective is to sign them up for TechShare," Mike said. "I'll try to look like an impressive VP of marketing and keep my mouth shut." *And I definitely want to see you coach another rep,* he thought. "What about our second call? I'd really like to understand how you strategize for high-level selling situations. You seem to be on a very different plane than others."

Tony looked down at his plate, then back to Mike. "Our second call is a tough one. I'm trying to save an account. They're planning to create an in-house system to manage product acquisition. They think they can cut costs if they build their own system that tests prices, places orders, tracks deliveries, and handles returns and credits. In other words, it would be a roll-your-own system that does some of the things that our TechShare program does. But it would treat our products, along with our competitors', as pure commodities, with price as the only real deciding factor. I need to change their thinking."

"You're in danger of losing some business?" Mike asked. "Considering your numbers and your record, I thought all you did was rain sales."

"Are you kidding?" Tony exclaimed. "Even if I can earn a customer's loyalty, I have to work hard to keep it. Never mind the fact

'Even if I can earn loyalty, I have to work hard to keep it.'

that we've got serious competitors who want loyal customers as badly as we do, and who are always trying to beat our prices, or forge better relationships, or both. Even when the competition isn't pressing me to come up with more creative solutions, the customers themselves are. In this case, my competition is the client's own technical staff."

He looked Mike in the eye. "*Action Selling* has made me a lot more effective. But if you think I know something that eliminates all my problems or allows me just to coast, you're going to be disappointed, Mike."

"Actually, I'm kind of relieved," Mike replied. "If your secret were a magic potion, I wouldn't be able to duplicate it or teach it to the rest of our sales force*." Also, I want to know more about how you troubleshoot and solve problems*, he thought. "Hey, here's the server. You want some coffee?"

The server cleared their plates and vanished in search of a coffeepot.

"Tell me about this client who worries you," Mike said.

Tony gathered his thoughts. "Well," he said, "my primary contact with them has been a woman named Carol. I've built a good relationship with her. Two weeks ago I called on her to talk about getting more of her business. My Commitment Objective was for her to agree to a primary-supplier arrangement similar to the one I got this morning from Janice.

"Ordinarily, Carol would have the authority to make that decision, but she has turned out to be the user-buyer in this picture," Tony continued. "The ultimate decision-maker is her boss, Bob. She told me that Bob is really excited about this roll-your-own idea. So I had to change my Commitment Objective and start working toward a meeting with Bob. He's the guy we'll call on today."

"Whoa," Mike said. "Walk me through the way you're handling the sales process. If Bob is the ultimate decision-maker, why were you presenting the primary-supplier deal only to Carol?"

'With customers that I rate as loyal, I have penetrated the account.'

"Okay," Tony said, backing up. "With all of my customers that I would rate as loyal, I've penetrated the account. I'm known in many areas of the company, not just with the procurement people. *Action Selling* points out that there are three distinct types of buyers who may be involved in a major sale, right? If you are going to sell loyalty, you need to have a solid relationship at all levels."

He pulled a pad out of his briefcase and made a few notes:

3 Buyer Types
Specialist   Measures   CIO = ?
                    Technical
                    Qualifications

User   Uses or   Dir Procure-
                    supervises users ment = Carol

UDM   Ultimate Decision CFO = Bob
                    Maker

Tony explained that "specialist buyers," in TechShare's situation, are people in Information Technology who will measure a software product's technical specifications and compatibility before anyone else in the company can install it.

"'User buyers" are people who will actually use the product—or, like Carol, people who manage the direct users. The "Ultimate Decision Maker," or UDM, is the person with final budget authority.

"The specialist buyer could be a sticky wicket in this case," Tony said, "because it's their CIO who might be my competition. I've met him, but don't plan to include him in this process. At least, not yet.

"Here's the other complication," he continued. "Up to this point in my dealings with her, Carol seemed to be the UDM. She has buying authority for products like ours. But since they consider this a mission-critical decision, Bob, the CFO, got involved. Two weeks ago, when I began presenting the primary-supplier deal to Carol, she told me that Bob is hot on the develop-your-own plan, and he has told her to 'take care of it.' So now Bob has suddenly stepped into the picture as the UDM. Of course, I can't rely on Carol to sell my solution upstairs. That's my job."

"All right, I'm with you so far," Mike said. "*Action Selling* also says that there are certain milestones in every sales process—critical steps that must be accomplished—and that Commitment Objectives are always tied to those milestones. How are you approaching this?"

"Good question," Tony said. "Before the call on Carol two weeks ago, my milestones had to do with analyzing her needs and her company's procurement process. In the meeting when she dropped the Bob bomb on me, the milestone I had reached was 'present primary-supplier proposal.' My Commitment Objective was to gain her agreement on it.

"When that exploded, the whole game changed," Tony continued. "Now my competition was the in-house system, so obviously I had to start looking for needs that TechShare might fill more effectively than the

> *'When the entire situation changed, you changed your Commitment Objective.'*

system they would build on their own. I decided to start with Carol's staff. So I changed my Commitment Objective to: 'Gain Carol's agreement to let me meet with her staff to completely understand their issues with product acquisition.'

In other words, Mike thought, *when the entire situation changed in the middle of a call, you immediately recognized that you needed a new game plan. So you changed your Commitment Objective, spun on a dime, and began working toward the new objective. And when you say that you "obviously" had to start looking for new needs to fill, you mean that you see nothing remarkable about what you did.*

Mike made a note:

Uses Commitment Objectives like a laser
Quick to redirect his selling game plan

Tony also had begun to draw again. "From the point when the roll-your-own system came up," he said, "my sales milestones looked like this."

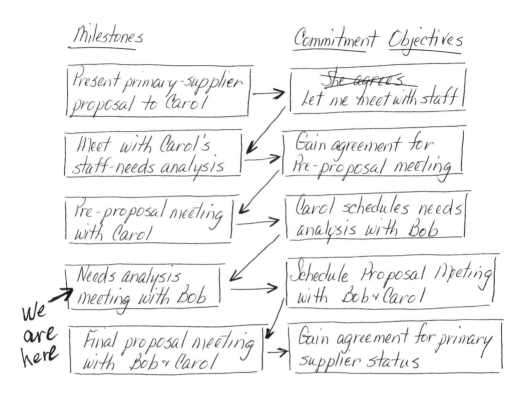

"So after I found out about the develop-your-own plan, I met with Carol's staff," Tony explained. "I asked questions that uncovered some serious concerns about how the in-house system could affect them and the company. Then I met with Carol and did a pre-proposal on how TechShare could address those concerns. Basically, it was, "Hey, Carol, based on what your people told me, I think there is a better solution, and here's why.'

"That pre-proposal got Carol leaning in my direction, so she arranged for me to meet with Bob," Tony continued. "Which brings us to today's call. Bob doesn't know me, but he knows that Carol and her people think I'm worth meeting with."

Mike nodded. "Which is why *Action Selling* tells you that all three types of buyers can be important and warns you never to ignore or brush off the user-buyers in your rush to get to the ultimate decision maker," he said.

"Loyalty runs deep into the customer's company," said Tony. "So anyway, today we'll call on Bob to analyze *his* needs for an

'Loyalty runs deep into the customer's company.'

effective and efficient product-acquisition system. I want an agreement to come back and present a full proposal to him and Carol. I want that proposal to blow the roll-your-own plan out of the water. But to do that, of course, I have to find out today what he really cares about."

"Or, in *Action Selling* terms," Mike said, "you need to discover his differentiated needs." *And I'll bet that's another part of your secret formula, Tony: you're really good at this,* he thought.

Mike sipped his coffee. "Let me see if I understand," he said. "You want to unsell Bob on the develop-your-own idea and sell him on a primary-supplier deal, with TechShare included. That's your purpose today"

"Not yet," Tony answered, adding a note that said 'We Are Here' to the milestone chart. "Here's what I plan to do: I want to end Act 3, 'Ask the Best Questions,' by gaining agreement on the needs I uncover, which is Act 4. Acts 5 and 6 will be focused on what he will learn by meeting with me again and how he'll be better off by hearing about my proposal. Asking for a commitment to meet again is Act 7. So that's what I want to accomplish today."

I thought I understood the Action Selling *system pretty well, but you live and breathe it; you are a master,* Mike thought. "Okay," he said, "but most of your preparation for this call has gone into the questions you'll ask Bob. Right?"

"Yes. It always is, Mike. Act 3 is where trust is built. And trust is the foundation of loyalty," Tony said.

> ***'Act 3 is where trust is built. And trust is the foundation of loyalty.'***

Tony's statement hit Mike like a pile of bricks. "Whoa, explain that to me."

Tony paused. *But trust is so fundamental to selling in a way that creates loyalty*, he thought. *How can I explain?* "All right," he said finally, "here's how I think about this. What motivates Bob? He's got this huge financial responsibility. That's what's driving the idea of a software system that treats products as commodities and purchasing as a commodity-acquisition process.

"But Bob also has internal customers to satisfy, right? He needs *their* loyalty. He needs them to trust and respect him. He doesn't want them to think he's a clueless jerk with no idea how their jobs work or how his new process might screw up their operations. I think that's the primary need I have to uncover."

"Hum," Mike hummed. *I believe I'm about to get an education*, he thought.

"If Bob wants loyalty from his people," Tony went on, "he has to earn their trust. They have to believe he acts in the best interests of the company and not just according to some agenda of his own. They have to believe he's on their side—that he respects them and listens to them and cares about what they need to do their jobs effectively. If he already knows that, fine. If he doesn't, I need to nudge him toward awareness of his need for the trust and loyalty of his people.

> *'When he knows I'm working for him, I'll have built the level of trust needed to earn his loyalty.'*

"If I want Bob to become loyal to *me*," Tony continued, "I have to earn his loyalty in exactly the same way. My Act 3 questions need to steer his thinking toward the conclusion that I'm not just a salesperson, I'm a solution. And not only a solution for the business's needs, though that's important, but for his personal issues. On a business *and* personal level, he needs a purchasing system that is effective, not just a cheap way to acquire products. And on a very personal level, he needs his people's loyalty. When he knows I'm working *for* him and that I've got something that can potentially get him where he personally wants to go, then I'll have built the level of trust needed to earn his loyalty."

Holy smoke, Tony, Mike thought, *your strategic thinking is somewhere beyond a master's level.* "I'd love to hear the questions that can accomplish that," he said.

"I'll tell you what I wrote down in my call prep for Act 3," Tony said. "But first, of course, there will have to be some Act 2 and some preliminary Act 3. Then I'll preface the questions that I have in store for him with something like this."

Tony began speaking as if Mike were the client. "As you know, Bob, I've met with Carol and had a separate meeting with the folks who are on the front lines working for her. We learned a lot of things that are going to help your company improve its processes. In fact, Carol told me that the meeting I had with her staff really got them thinking about how to make the company operate better and at the same time solve some of the frustrations that they were having."

Tony looked at his call-prep notes. "That leads up to the the first question I wrote: Bob, when ideas that can actually improve the company's financial performance are generated by the employees who are stakeholders in the solution, how much importance do you place on trying to find a way to implement their ideas?"

Mike almost choked on his coffee. "Oh my, Tony," he said. "I can imagine his answer. And I bet he'll be awfully hungry to hear your solution."

"He'll need to invest in another meeting to have that meal," said Tony with a smile.

He looked at his watch. "Hey, speaking of meals, ours is running long. We'd better go meet George."

For a moment, Mike looked blank.

"Remember George?" Tony asked. "The other sales rep who wants my help? Our next call? I got so caught up in talking about my own client that I almost forgot about him."

Chapter 4

FROM PROBLEM SOLVER TO BUSINESS PARTNER

The customer need that never goes away.

George's client's building had a spacious lobby area, its furniture arranged into several conversation pits. As he had promised, George arrived early and staked out a spot for them to meet. It was a perfect setting for their pre-call meeting.

After a little Act 2 relationship-building talk, Tony got straight to business. "What's your Commitment Objective for the call, and how would you like us to help?" he asked George.

"I want them to agree to sign up for our loyalty program, TechShare," George answered. "The ultimate decision maker and two key influencers will be in our meeting."

He turned to Mike. "I've already talked to Tony about these clients. I really want to lock them up on this. I'm glad you're able to come along on the call, Mike, because TechShare is your baby, and your presence will demonstrate that we take their business seriously.

"As for you, Tony," George continued, "I told them that you're our No. 1 guru on implementing TechShare. I'd like you to help me present it to them. I want us to tag-team them on Acts 5 and 6—Sell the Company and Sell the Product—so that we walk out of there with a committed, loyal customer. As for how we'll do it, exactly, that's why I wanted this pre-meeting."

George seems bright, capable, and professional, Mike thought, *and he talks in* Action Selling *terms just like Tony does. Come on, Tony, show me what you know but solid reps like George don't. Save my job, buddy. Help me resurrect TechShare.*

Tony leaned forward in his chair to answer George. "Wait, back up," he said. "I want to question your basic premise. You're saying we'll turn these clients into loyal customers if we can sell them TechShare—because it's our loyalty program. I'd say that's backwards. First you have to sell them loyalty. *Then* maybe you can sell them our loyalty program."

'First you have to sell them loyalty. Then maybe you can sell them our loyalty program.'

George looked blank. He glanced at Mike, but got no help. "What do you mean?" he asked.

Tony smiled at him. "You and the other reps in the office have asked me how I sell so many TechShare programs. But I could never articulate my so-called secret until Mike started to prod me about the relationship between loyalty *programs* and loyal customers. Now I'm getting a better handle on it.

"George, the fact that I sell a lot of TechShare programs is almost incidental. It's like a symptom, not a cause. My customers don't become loyal because I'm good at selling a loyalty program. They buy TechShare because I'm good at selling loyalty."

George flicked his eyes nervously to Mike again. *Don't embarrass me in front of a vice president, Tony,* he thought. *What are you talking about?*

"Don't worry, you know this already," Tony assured him. "You just don't know you know it. This is what the Five Buying Decisions are all about if you simply take them to their logical conclusion. In any sales situation, the first thing the customer must decide to buy is the salesperson, right? Well, on a pedestrian level, that means clients are satisfied with you—maybe even pleased. But on what Mike calls the master's level, it means your customers become loyal. They trust you. They see you as a valuable asset. They'd much rather deal with you. In fact, they stop shopping."

Tony was getting onto a roll. "How strongly do you believe that if you want to sell a product, you first have to sell yourself, then sell your company?"

"I absolutely believe it," George answered. "That's fundamental to *Action Selling*. It's made me a much more effective salesperson. But…"

> *'At the Master's level, customers become loyal. They stop shopping.'*

"No 'but's,'" Tony interrupted. "TechShare is a product, George, it isn't 'loyalty.' Mike gave it tangible features and benefits. It's become a great product, like all of our products. So, it's another example of 'what' we sell, right?"

"Sure, I understand that," said George.

"Loyalty is more about 'how' we sell than 'what' we sell," Tony said. "Increased loyalty should be the ultimate outcome of every single sales call.

'Loyalty is more about 'how' we sell than 'what' we sell.'

"Here's how I see it," he continued. "Customers will buy products from you without necessarily being loyal; they only have to be satisfied. However, they probably won't bind themselves to our company with a loyalty *program* like TechShare unless they've become loyal to you first—to *you*, the salesperson.

"I couldn't tell you my secret because I didn't realize until today that it was a secret. You want to know how I sell so many TechShare

'Increased loyalty should be the ultimate outcome of every single sales call.'

programs? It's because my underlying goal is never just to sell TechShare. What I try to sell is loyalty—to *me*, first of all, then to my company. If I can do that, and if the client's situation is appropriate, then TechShare usually just rides along like a passenger on a train. I'll say it again: *A loyalty program is not loyalty.* It's only a comprehensive way for customers to *act* on the loyalty we've already built."

Mike saw George's eyes widen in understanding and realized his own eyes were doing the same. *There it is!* he thought. *That's what Tony has been trying to tell me.*

Mike scratched some notes:

Satisfied ≠ Loyal

Loyalty Program ≠ Loyalty

George, meanwhile, had been absorbing Tony's speech. "I think I get what you're saying," he said finally. "But I've become a lot better at 'how' I sell, since we got the training. And I mean a *lot* better. Yet you obviously do something that I don't to take your clients from 'satisfied' to 'loyal.' What is it? And how will I do it in the call we're about to make?"

"I've been wondering about that while Mike and I talked," Tony said. "I have a hunch, so bear with me for a minute. *Action Selling* describes three roles that every effective salesperson has to play, regardless of the system he's using. The first one is 'orchestrator.' That means leveraging resources and coordinating

> **The first role is Orchestrator.**

selling activities in ways that demonstrate how the salesperson's relationships and the resources of the salesperson's company can provide good solutions for the customer. You're being an orchestrator by bringing Mike and me along on this call. How else have you demonstrated orchestration skills for this client?"

George hardly had to think about his answer. "I set up all of their users with tech support on the speed dial of their phones," he said. "They love that. Some of them call it the 'Bat Phone to the Commissioner.' Also, I organized a special training event for my key accounts in this client's industry. I brought in an expert speaker to talk about trends in their market. They attended, and they were happy with it."

The second role is Consultant.

Well, I'm impressed, Mike thought, wondering how many reps had thought of the Bat Phone idea.

"Sounds like you have the orchestrator base covered," Tony said, sounding impressed himself. "What about the other two roles a salesperson has to play?"

"The second one is 'consultant,'" George answered.

"Right," Tony said. "How have you acted as a consultant with this client?"

"I'm pretty good at diagnosing problems that come up, I think, and I've helped these people with some," George replied. "The speed-dial idea was my solution for their concerns about access to technical knowledge. And I suggested a change to their ordering process that helped to smooth out an inventory problem."

"How do you learn about these kinds of problems?" Tony asked.

"Mainly by asking questions," George said. "It's all about Act 3. Sometimes I think of myself as a doctor and the client as a patient. If I ask them, 'Where does it hurt?' in the right way, they usually tell me."

Mike liked George's answer, but he was starting to despair. *George knows the* Action Selling *process, and he follows it. So where does he fall short, Tony? Where are you going with this?*

Tony, on the other hand, looked energized, as if something

George said had confirmed his hunch. "Okay, that's 'consultant,'" he said to George. "And the third role?"

> ## *The third role is Relationship Builder.*

"I don't remember," George confessed.

"The third role is 'long-term relationship builder,'" Tony said.

"Oh, yeah, that's it."

Tony smiled as if the mystery were solved. "Yes, George, I think maybe that *is* it. That may be the thing I do that you don't. Because instead of 'long-term relationship builder,' that third role just as easily could be called 'loyalty builder.'"

George and Mike both goggled at him. "Explain that, please," Mike said.

Tony laughed, delighted. "I think we've discovered what you came here to find out, Mike. At least, it's a big part of the answer. The rela-tionship-builder role is about consis-tency in using the *Action Selling* sys-tem. It's about working through the

> ## *'The relationship-builder role is about consistency using Action Selling.'*

process with the client over time, *every* time. That applies especial-ly to Act 3—Asking the Best Questions to uncover the customer's needs. But there's more to 'needs' than just specific problems you can help the customer solve.

"George, you said you feel like a doctor when you're doing Act 3. You try to find out where the customer hurts. That's a great description of the 'consultant' role, and it's important. But it's only the first step. It's essentially reactive. To build extreme trust and loyalty, you have to move beyond that. You have to become proactive. If a customer's arteries are blocked, recommend surgery. But then

'To build extreme trust, you have to be proactive.'

start practicing preventative medicine."

"What do you mean?" asked George and Mike almost in unison.

Good question, Tony thought. *How do I explain this?* "All right, look," he said. "What is every client's greatest ongoing need, the need that never goes away? It's to keep getting better at what they do, right? They need to keep getting better to remain competitive. They need to keep getting better to become leaders in their industries or to stay in the leadership position."

Tony was struck by a sudden thought. "For instance, why is

'Every client's greatest need is to keep getting better.'

Mike sitting here with us right now?" he asked. He turned to address Mike. "You solved a huge problem, scored a huge success, and

became a corporate hero when you introduced *Action Selling*. But did all your problems go away? No. Now you need the sales force to get even better, and you have to figure out how.

"It never ends," Tony continued. "Not for Mike, and not for any

'A customer who trusts your ongoing commitment to help improve their business will be a loyal customer.'

customer you'll ever have. Do you want to create real loyalty? Solve problems, yes, but then *keep going*.

Keep digging for ways to help clients build their businesses. Don't just be a doctor they call when they're sick. Be a proactive business partner. Be like a personal coach who never stops trying to help them with their need that never goes away—the need to *keep getting better* at what they do. A customer who trusts your ongoing commitment to help improve their business will be a loyal customer.

"That's what I think the 'long-term relationship builder' role is about," Tony said. "Heck, that's exactly what we mean when we say we want 'loyal' customers, isn't it? We mean we want customers who are willing—no, eager—to form long-term relationships with us. That's what our competitors want, too, regardless of how they sell. We've just got a better system for achieving it—if only we use the system consistently.

"Loyalty isn't TechShare, guys," he concluded. "Loyalty is a long-term relationship, with or without TechShare involved. But if our salespeople build loyalty first, TechShare often will follow."

Bingo! Mike thought, scribbling notes furiously.

Relationship builder = Loyalty builder

Reactive salesperson = Satisfied customer

Proactive salesperson = Loyal customer

Need that never ends = Business improvement

George took a while to think. "That makes a lot of sense, Tony," he said finally. "Does this mean I've got the wrong Commitment Objective for the call? Should I not try to gain their agreement to sign up for TechShare?"

"No, I don't mean that," Tony said. "A Commitment Objective requires the customer to agree to take some specific action. Loyalty isn't an action. It's a necessary foundation for the action you want the customer to take. From what you've told me, TechShare would work very well for this client. So I think that's still our Commitment Objective. The question is, how will you build a sufficient loyalty foundation to achieve it? Which is just another way of saying…"

> *'Loyalty isn't an action. It's a necessary foundation for the action you want the customer to take.'*

George jumped in to finish Tony's sentence. "Which is another way of saying, 'How does a salesperson sell himself?'" he said. "And that starts with Asking the Best Questions and listening carefully to the answers."

"See? You do know this already," Tony said. "Okay, we want to be able to demonstrate to these clients that we're not just here to sell them something, and we're not just here to bandage their flesh wounds, either. What questions will position our TechShare presentation so we can demonstrate our commitment to help drive their business forward over the long haul?"

George, Tony, and Mike all jumped in excitedly, throwing out possibilities, George filling in Mike when necessary on the customer's situation. They settled on three key questions for George to ask the clients, with a preliminary question to set the stage for asking each of them.

Mike wrote down the three questions, along with their lead-ins.

'Business Partner' Loyalty Questions

1. How do you position your company against your competitors?
How much importance do you place on working with suppliers that can tangibly impact your competitive position?

2. When it comes to product procurement, what are your company's long-term goals?
What are the consequences of not reaching these goals?

3. In addition to the actual cost of a product, what other costs do you consider when you calculate Total Acquisition Cost?
How interested would you be in working with a supplier that has a better solution for managing Total Acquisition Cost?

"Hey, it's time to meet the clients," George said. "Tony, Mike, thanks to both of you. I think you just showed me how to take my game to a whole new level."

"The thanks belong to Tony," Mike said, as they rose and walked toward the elevator. "I'm not done picking your brain yet, Tony, but I feel 10 years younger than I did this morning. Let's go sell a TechShare program."

"Amen," said George. "But first let's sell some loyalty."

Chapter 5

THE RIGHT LEVER CAN
MOVE THE WORLD

You can see loyalty happen.

The call on George's customers ran longer than expected, so Mike and Tony had to rush to make their next appointment on time. They said goodbye to a jubilant George, scheduled a debriefing conference call with him for the next day, and sped off to Bob's office.

Bob was pleasant enough during the introductions. Tony made a point of presenting Mike as a high-level executive, and Bob was gracious, though not overly impressed. But they had no more than settled into their chairs when Bob opened the meeting with a line that made Mike's blood run cold.

"Carol told me you have some ideas for us, and I'll listen to your pitch," he said. "In fairness, though, I should tell you that we have a talented group of software developers, and I've pretty much decided we'll take care of this purchasing-system project ourselves. I've only got about 20 minutes, so let's get started."

Holy smoke, Tony, you weren't kidding about this call being a tough one, Mike thought. *We're dead on arrival. What now?*

> ## '90 percent of our salespeople would have given the client what he asked for: a product pitch.'

Tony, however, seemed unflustered. "We appreciate you giving us the time, Bob. Carol has told me a little bit about your role in the company. May I ask how you developed your interest in business finance?"

The query surprised Bob, and he stopped to think. It obviously wasn't something he got to discuss often. "That's a good question," he said. And Bob began to talk—about himself. Tony listened attentively.

There's my answer to, "What now?" Mike thought. *We're in Act 2, so we stay in Act 2, building a personal relationship. I'll bet 90 percent of our salespeople would have thrown the system out the window and given the client what he asked for: a product pitch. We're probably still doomed, but at least the guy is talking.*

Tony asked Bob a few more questions about his background and his role in the company. Bob began to loosen up a bit as he answered. He may have been no closer to changing his mind, at least consciously. *But he's becoming engaged in the conversation*, Mike observed. *This isn't what he expected.*

Tony moved seamlessly into Act 3 by mentioning his previous meetings with Carol and her staff. He asked questions based on concerns he had uncovered. Bob clearly was impressed by the research Tony had done, and his answers grew more candid. He began to think out loud, working his way through some of the issues Carol's people had raised.

Bob seriously cares about making the right decision on the pur-chasing system, Mike realized. *He'd be deaf to a sales pitch from someone trying to talk him out of his grow-your-own plan, but he doesn't mind discussing his situation with someone who seems to understand many of the issues involved—and who also seems to care.*

Then Tony asked the question he had revealed to Mike at lunch: "Bob, if your people come up with solid ideas that will improve business operations, how much importance do you place on trying to implement those ideas?'"

"Well, I try to find ways to empower our employees so they'll feel invested in what the company is doing and how," Bob replied. "People buy in when they're involved in decision-making."

"When they buy in," Tony asked, "how does that affect a pro-ject's success?"

"It's huge! Employees can make or break a project depending on whether they buy in."

"This is a subject that really interests me," Tony said. "I'm curi-ous about your opinion. When employees feel invested, as you say, how does that affect their loyalty to your company?"

That question obviously touched on a key concern of Bob's, and he began to talk about it, growing more passionate as he spoke. His resistance had been thawing, but now it seemed to Mike as if a dam had broken.

You can see loyalty start to form, Mike thought. *You can actually watch it happen!* Bob's body language changed. The whole context of the conversation changed. It was like night and day. *He has stopped seeing Tony as a guy trying to sell him something,* Mike realized. *Now he just wants to dig in and figure out a better way to do things—with our help.*

> **'You can see loyalty start to form. You can actually watch it happen!'**

Mike tried to listen with the same attention Tony was showing, but his mind wanted to process what he was seeing. *When we walked in, Bob was seriously invested in his grow-your-own scheme for purchasing management. He wouldn't have met with us at all if Carol hadn't prodded him. He expected us to try to sell him out of his plan. Now he's discovering that Tony has questions instead of just preconceived answers—and that the questions are informed by research Tony already did with his people. The game has changed. This is no longer just a sales call. Bob has started talking to us as if we're his business partners. It's like we're now on his team, working together to decide how his operation could become more effective.*

Mike realized that he had seen a similar change come over George's clients in their previous call. *I wasn't as attuned to it, but it was all there, including the change in body language. They were ready to buy TechShare before we actually presented it—because they had bought us. And not just on a 'satisfied' level, but on the 'loyalty' level. They wanted us on their team.* He smiled, remembering George's delight after the successful call.

Mike snapped back into the present conversation when Bob

stopped talking abruptly, as if catching himself on the verge of saying something he shouldn't. He had been talking about preparing for
"changing circumstances."

Something big and hush-hush is in the works at this company,
Mike thought. *You were about to talk out of school to Tony, weren't
you, Bob, just like Janice did this morning when she discussed the
secret acquisition. And on the first call!*

Tony hesitated for a second and made a note, then tactfully
dropped the point about "changing circumstances" and asked another question about what the purchasing situation looked like from
Bob's point of view. *Good decision*, Mike thought. *Don't press him
for insider information until you've built more trust. In fact, you're
probably building trust by refusing to press.*

The 20 minutes Bob allotted for their meeting had become 45,
without Bob minding at all, when Tony did a quick Act 4, agreeing
with Bob on the major needs they had identified. Then Tony moved
on to Act 5, telling a short version of his company story.

"Bob, you said you put a high priority on empowerment so that
your employees feel invested," Tony said. "My company's management feels the same way. That's exactly why our sales-consulting
process includes meetings with people who use our products, like
Carol's folks, and not just with people at the management level. It
gives us a far better understanding of our clients' needs before we
start trying to figure out solutions."

He pointed at Mike. "Mike is the executive who pushed hardest
to make user meetings a regular part of our process."

That's my cue, Mike thought, recognizing the demonstration of "orchestration" skills as Tony positioned him as a resource that made their company a good match for Bob's. As Bob turned to him

> **'My sales force should be doing that...They're always in such a rush to get to the decision maker.'**

with new interest, Mike spoke briefly about his conviction that people at all levels of a company are likely to have valuable insights into the organization's problems and opportunities.

"You know, *my* sales force should be doing that," Bob said thoughtfully. "They're always in such a rush to get straight to the top decision maker. I think they miss a lot of important information."

Good idea, Mike thought. *And I'll bet it's one that never crossed your mind before. See, partner? We're already a great resource for your company.* He noticed Tony smiling, as if sharing the same thought.

Tony moved to Act 6, speaking briefly about the TechShare program and why he thought it might be a good alternative to address Bob's key concerns. Then he started to wrap things up. *TFBR,* Mike thought, recognizing the structure of Tony's next comments. *Tie-back, Feature, Benefit, Reaction.*

"You've given us some extra time, Bob, and we appreciate it. But we don't want to mess up your schedule too badly. I'm sure you'd like to look at all the best options available," Tony said, tying back the conversation to a point upon which Bob had agreed earlier. "I can document the things we've talked about, as well as what I learned about your situation from my meetings with Carol and her staff." (*Feature*, Mike thought.) "That will give you a complete needs analysis so you can easily evaluate your financial options."

(*Benefit,* Mike thought. *Now ask him for a reaction.*) "How do you see that helping you?"

"I think that would help all of us get on the same page," Bob answered.

"Good. I'll prepare the analysis and my recommendation, put it into a proposal, and come back and present it to you and Carol. I know that she has next Tuesday morning available. How does Tuesday at 9 a.m. look for you?"

"That will work," Bob said. "I'll look forward to it."

Cha-ching! Mike thought. *You just accomplished your Commitment Objective to get the proposal meeting, Tony. I didn't think you had a prayer.*

Mike restrained himself until they left Bob's office and climbed back into the car to head for the airport. "That went pretty well, I think," Tony said in deliberate understatement.

"Pretty well? *Pretty* well? Hoo-hah!" Mike began hand-drumming on the dashboard and stomping his feet in celebration. "I've never seen a sales call turn around like that!"

Tony laughed as he started the car and pulled out of their parking space. "Yeah, that was one for the books," he said, letting his excitement show. "Do you want to know when I felt we were really over the hump and that he was seeing us as potential business partners? It was when you explained why you believe salespeople should talk to employees at different levels of a company, and he said, '*My* sales force should be doing that.' I owe you for that one, Mike."

"Do you want to know what jumped out for me about that call?" Mike asked. "Wait a second, I want to write this down." He held up his notes.

Stick with the system. Consistency!

You can SEE loyalty start to happen

Orchestrator → consultant → relationship builder

Your company story: It's a loyalty tool. Use it!

You use the system—it doesn't use you

"First," Mike explained, "you didn't let Bob push you straight into Act 6 with that business about, 'Let's hear your pitch in 20 minutes.' You knew the conversation belonged in Act 2, and that's where you kept it. That was the moment when you gave us a fighting chance to save the call.

"What really amazed me, though, was that I could actually see

'I could actually see Bob turn from a resistant customer into a trusting business partner.'

Bob start to turn from a resistant customer into a trusting business partner. I saw the change in him as his perception of *you* changed. You were a salesperson to him, then you were a consultant and orchestrator, and then you were a relationship builder. I watched loyalty happen! I could see it and sense it and feel it.

"You recognize the signs, don't you Tony—the changes in body language and attitude, the whole feel of the conversation? I'll bet you look for those signs to guide you and keep you on the right track instead of running up dead-end alleys."

"Sure," Tony agreed. "You can absolutely see trust and loyalty happen. It goes back to the five major buying decisions. When the customer's buying decisions are being made in the proper sequence, the loyalty meter rises." Tony gestured with his hand, indicating five consecutive higher levels. "Loyalty is an intangible quality, but it's a tangible force when you're using a communications process that follows the customer's decision process."

> *'When the customer's buying decisions are being made in the proper sequence, the loyalty meter rises.'*

Mike nodded, his assumption confirmed. "You also impressed me by using your company story to tie into his feelings about empowerment and involvement. I don't believe that most of our reps recognize what a powerful loyalty tool their company story can be. I know I didn't fully appreciate it until now."

Tony's eyes left the road for a glance at Mike's list. "What's that last note about?"

"I'm not sure how to express it," Mike said. "Since I'm familiar with *Action Selling,* I knew you were using the system. I could identify the steps and the processes. But I could never *catch* you following steps or using techniques, if you know what I mean. Nothing was forced or unnatural. You never seemed like a salesperson following a formula—or even like a consultant following one."

Mike reached for an image to capture what he was trying to convey. "It was like watching Fred Astaire dance," he said finally. "No

'I use the system, it doesn't use me.'

matter how much work went into the choreography, he always seemed perfectly natural. He never seemed to be *trying*. You came across the same way. I guess 'genuine' is the word. You were always just…you."

"I think I know what you mean," Tony said. "But that's the way the system works. It doesn't ask me to try to *be* somebody else. It just gives me some skills to use and an effective framework for managing the sales process, including the relationships involved. It doesn't replace my thinking or my creativity. It isn't a box that I have to squeeze into. Instead it leverages whatever talents and abilities I bring to the table. So, yes, I like the way you put it: I use the system, it doesn't use me."

They reached the departures level of the airport and Tony pulled to the curb. "Did you get what you came for, Mike?" he asked. "This all seems pretty straightforward to me. I still don't feel as if I revealed any deep secrets about trust or loyalty."

"Ah, but you did, Tony. I think you've given me several. If I can put it all together and communicate it to the sales force in the right way, I have a hunch our business is going to take another giant leap forward."

They climbed out of the car and shook hands. "Thanks, Tony. I mean it," Mike said. "You've shown me a way to make the company grow. I understand why your clients are so loyal to you. I feel the same way. You're not just one of our salespeople. You're more like … a trusted business partner," he smiled. "You've helped me with the need that never goes away—the need to get better at what I do."

Tony shook his head. "The fact is, Mike, I should thank you. I'm not some natural-born, superstar salesperson. You handed me the loyalty lever when you introduced the system. Who was it that said with the right lever, he could move the world? All I do is grab onto that lever and never let go."

Epilogue

Mike sells some loyalty.

"So, you think you've figured out how to salvage your TechShare program?" asked Neil, Mike's CEO.

TechShare is 'my' program, is it? Mike thought. *The Action Selling system I introduced doubled our growth rate, so that's 'ours.' TechShare tanked, so it's mine. Why doesn't this surprise me?*

But Mike pushed that thought aside in favor of a more pressing one: *Oh, no you don't, Neil. You're asking me to present you with my solution—to make a pitch. Thanks to a certain master-level salesperson in Arizona, I know better. We're at the stage where I ask the questions and you'll do most of the talking. But I will give you a teaser, just to let you know that this won't be an ordinary conversation.*

"Like I said when I asked for this meeting, I have some ideas," Mike replied. "I'd like to get your thinking on them. You know about my trip to Phoenix, right?"

"You were going out there to see Tony, the sales rep who has sold 10 times more TechShare programs than anybody else."

"About 10 times more than our average reps, yes."

"And you learned his secret?" Neil asked. "You know why he's so much better at selling your loyalty program?"

"I think so," Mike replied. "His secret is that he's *not* any better at selling loyalty programs. What he's better at selling is loyalty." *There's your teaser, Neil*, he thought. *Now ask me what on earth I'm talking about.*

Neil stared at Mike for a long moment. "Explain that to me."

"That's where I'd like to get your input," Mike replied. "I wonder if we've been going at this backwards." *Note the 'we,' Neil*, he thought. "We call TechShare a loyalty program, but what is it that we really want the program to accomplish?"

"Same as any loyalty program," Neil said, impatiently. "What we *wanted*"(he stressed the past tense, with an unfriendly look at Mike) "was to give customers some technology that would lock them in so we'd get more of their business. TechShare was supposed to make us their supplier of first choice."

"Here's one thing that I learned," Mike said. "If they give us most of their business because we package some attractive technology and offer them a good deal on our products, we're still vulnerable to any competitor who devises a comparable package. Neil, how would you describe an ideal level of loyalty—

'How would you describe an ideal level of loyalty?'

something that goes beyond 'supplier of first choice until somebody offers me the next choice?'"

Neil found the question intriguing. He thought about it. "Well, I guess the ideal would be that they're so satisfied with us that they stop looking around for better deals. They stop shopping. 'Satisfied' wouldn't even be the right word.

> *'They're so satisfied with us that they stop looking around for better deals.'*

Ideally, loyal customers wouldn't just figure that buying from us is the path of least resistance or whatever. They would actively *want* to do business with us and with nobody else."

"I agree," Mike said. *And I notice you're starting to forget to remind me that I'm to blame for TechShare,* he thought. "Satisfaction isn't enough. In fact, I found some research showing that 75 percent of customers who leave a company for a competitor say that they were 'satisfied' or even 'very satisfied' with the company they left. Neil, you've been a customer for all kinds of companies. When you think of suppliers who pleased you so much that you stopped shopping—and I'll bet there weren't many of them—what was it that made you feel that way?"

> *'When you think of suppliers who pleased you so much that you stopped shopping, what was it that made you feel that way?'*

Neil considered the question for a full minute, remembering his experiences as a customer. "I can think of two," he said, finally. "One was a business-to-business situation, the other was a gardening service I used when I lived in Maryland. But it wasn't the companies, as such, that made me feel unusually loyal. In both cases it was an individual: one salesperson and one gardener."

"What did the salesperson do, specifically, that made you stop shopping?"

'I trusted her. She actually seemed to care.'

"She didn't act like a damned salesperson," Neil said, laughing. "I wouldn't say it in front of our reps, but it's true."

Maybe that's exactly what we should say to our reps, Mike thought. "How did she act?" he asked.

"I don't know how to describe it," Neil said. "I mean, she was a salesperson, pure and simple, but she acted more like a consultant or, I don't know, a…"

"Business partner?" Mike suggested.

"Yeah, that was the feeling. I trusted her. She actually seemed to care about my operation, and she tried to help me improve it. She was a good listener and a good sounding board. I remember she once brought in one of her technical experts to help me think through a major project even though her company could only handle a small piece of it—and that was *if* I even gave them the business. I did give her the business, of course. I wish I could have given her the whole project."

'She acted like a consultant and an orchestrator. Beyond that, she built a strong personal relationship.'

"So she acted like a consultant and an orchestrator, coordinating resources and expertise on your behalf?" Mike asked. "And beyond that, she built a strong personal relationship with you, based on your trust that she wasn't just there to sell you things but was committed to helping you improve your business and get better at doing the things you needed to do. Is that right?"

Neil sat back in his chair and regarded Mike, struck by a thought. "Holy smoke. I haven't by any chance just described Tony in Phoenix, have I?"

"To a tee," Mike said, looking Neil straight in the eyes. "You want to know what else I learned in Arizona, Neil? I learned that there's nothing wrong with our loyalty program. But there was something wrong with the way I thought about it—the way we all thought about it. A loyalty program is just another product—or a bundle of services. Loyalty itself is some-

> *'People become loyal to other people.'*

thing deeper, richer and much more valuable. Tony's customers don't become loyal to us because they buy TechShare. And they don't buy TechShare from Tony because he knows some secret way to sell this particular program. People become loyal to other *people*, the way you became loyal to that saleswoman. The reason Tony's clients buy TechShare is because they first buy Tony."

Neil nodded along, intensely interested. The atmosphere of the meeting had changed completely, Mike noticed. *We're teammates now, working to solve a problem. Whoever that saleswoman was, God bless her. Thanks to her, you know what I'm talking about, Neil.*

"But wait a minute," Neil said. "Isn't that a basic part of the *Action Selling* system? The buyer's first decision is whether to buy the salesperson. Shouldn't our reps already know that?"

"They do, but they don't," Mike said. "I mean, yes, the answer is right there, but most reps don't quite get it, any more than I did.

They still think in terms of 'selling' and 'satisfaction,' assigning genuine loyalty to the realm of special programs that have to be sold. They don't see what Tony saw intuitively: Carried to its logical conclusion, our selling system is also a communication system—and a blueprint for building loyalty. A loyalty program is just

'Our selling system is a blueprint for building loyalty.'

a convenient way for customers to *act* on the loyalty a salesperson first has to build. My mistake—our mistake—has been to think of TechShare as our major weapon in the battle for customer loyalty. Wrong. Our primary weapons in that battle are our individual salespeople. Loyalty first, loyalty programs second." *And I'm talking too much*, he thought. *Ask a question.*

"Let me ask you another question," Mike said. "Suppose all of our sales reps got a lot better at building relationships like the one you had with that saleswoman—and like the ones Tony has with his clients. What do you think that would mean in terms of the loyalty we earn from our customers? What would it mean for our growth objectives if our whole sales force knew how to take their clients beyond the 'satisfaction' level and move them to the 'stop shopping' level?"

'Tony is extremely loyal to our company.'

"Are you kidding?" Neil said, imagining not Tony, whom he had never seen in action, but a small army of reps like his favorite saleswoman. "That would be huge. So what are you suggesting? Do you want us to hire new people? Or create a major behavior change in the reps we've got?"

Not quite yet, Mike thought. "I'll get to that," he said. "Another thing that struck me about Tony is that he's extremely loyal to our company. That really comes across when he talks to clients about us. What do you think about the connection between employee loyalty and the employee's ability to create loyalty in customers?"

"I'm sure there's a strong connection," Neil answered. "If I don't feel much loyalty to the company I work for, it would be awfully tough to convince you to feel any. And I think that my own sense of loyalty to my company would be hard to fake."

"In your opinion Neil, what kinds of things can a company do to gain loyalty from its own employees?"

"That's an awfully big question," Neil said, mulling it over. "But I think that one key loyalty builder is for employees to feel as if they're growing in their careers. The biggest reason employees leave a company is because they feel they are in dead-end jobs."

"I agree," Mike said. "That was a big issue for Tony. He told me how much he appreciated the training we gave him. How do you think that kind of investment pays off in terms of creating loyal employees, who in turn are more likely to create loyal customers?"

Neil laughed. "You want to do something to improve our reps' ability to build better customer relationships, don't you, Mike? Relax, partner, you've already convinced me you're onto something big here. Maybe something enormous. What do you want to do? How would it work?"

Did you just call me 'partner'? Mike thought. *It's time for Act 4.* "First let me be sure we're on the same page," he said. "Since reps like Tony can sell TechShare very well, the lack of success is likely due to the way others approach selling it. Stronger personal relationships with a sales rep lead to more success in selling loyalty programs. Greater loyalty in our employees is a prerequisite to generating loyalty in our customers. Do you think that assessment is correct, Neil?"

"Yes. We've been over and over TechShare, and I'm convinced it's at least as good as any other loyalty program in our industry. I know I've been rough on you, Mike, but I could never see where we screwed up in creating the actual program. That's been part of my frustration."

Mike was struck by the "we" in "We screwed up." *Now, that's a buying signal*, he thought. *On to Acts 6 and 7.*

"Here's what I recommend," Mike said. "I'd like another meeting, in two weeks, with you and the regional vice presidents. At that meeting, I want to propose additional training for all of our sales reps. My tentative title for it is 'Masters in *Action Selling*.' It will focus on how to sell loyalty—that is, how to sell loyalty first and TechShare second. Its theme will be that loyalty is always being gained or lost in the course of every single sales call, and that a salesperson's overriding responsibility is always to sell loyalty. Everything we do needs to be connected to increasing loyalty. If we do that, TechShare will follow. I'll be prepared to describe the training, its goals, and how it will work."

Mike took a breath. *Gaining your agreement for that proposal meeting is my Commitment Objective for this call, Neil.* So here goes:

"How does that sound?" he asked.

ORDER MORE BOOKS!

  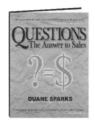 

TO ORDER BOOKS:

• Call (800) 232-3485	$19.95 Retail
• www.ActionSelling.com	3.00 Discount
• Fax (763) 473-0109	$16.95 Reader Price
• Mail to The Sales Board	

QUANTITY	BOOK	BOOK ORDER FORM
☐	Action Selling	**SHIPPING AND HANDLING**
☐	Selling Your Price	$3.95 per US order
☐	Questions: The Answer to Sales	Can/Int'l actual cost
☐	Masters of Loyalty	Payable in US funds

BILL MY CREDIT CARD

THE SALES BOARD
15200 25ᵀᴴ AVE. N.
PLYMOUTH, MN 55447

Card# _____ Exp. ____

DISC ____ VISA____ MC ____ AMEX____

Signature _____

Bill to _____	# of Books _____
Address _____	Price $ 16.95
City _____ ST ___ Zip ___	Total $_____
Daytime phone _____	MN Sales Tax $_____
Ship to _____	Ship/Handling $ 3.95
Address _____	Total Due $_____
City _____ ST ___ Zip ___	

Please allow 5-7 days for US Delivery. Can/Int'l orders pleas allow 10 days.
This offer is subject to change without notice

GET TRAINED AND CERTIFIED AS AN *ACTION SELLING* PROFESSIONAL!

Want to learn more about how Action Selling can help your organization realize its full sales potential? For information about training and certification for yourself or your salespeople, contact The Sales Board.

Founded in 1990, The Sales Board has boosted the performance of more than 2,500 companies and 300,000 salespeople worldwide in virtually every industry. Action Selling provides a systematic approach to managing and conducting the entire sales process. Our complete training program provides all the necessary tools for students and instructors. Training is customized specifically for each organization's selling situation and even for individual salespeople.

Studies document that veteran salespeople who become Action Selling Certified improve their sales performance by an annual average of 16 percent. As for rookie salespeople, there is no finer system to start them off on the right foot and make them productive immediately.

Students participate in a highly interactive two-day training session facilitated by our talented trainers or by their own Action Selling Certified managers. Students then take part in Skill Drills to refine and reinforce their new skills in the field. Accountability is built into the process with management reinforcement, plus an assessment and certification system.

To learn more about the complete Action Selling training and certification system, please contact us or visit our Web site:

The Sales Board
(800) 232-3485
info@thesalesboard.com
www.TheSalesBoard.com

ABOUT THE AUTHOR

Duane Sparks is chairman and founder of The Sales Board, a Minneapolis-based company that has trained and certified more than 300,000 salespeople in the system and the skills of Action Selling. He is the author of the Best Selling book, *Action Selling, How to sell like a professional even if you think you are one* and *Selling Your Price, How to escape the race to the bargain basement and Questions: The Answer to Sales.*

In a 30-year career as a salesperson and sales manager, Duane has sold products ranging from office equipment to insurance. He was the top salesperson at every company he ever worked for. He developed Action Selling while owner of one of the largest computer marketers in the United States. Even in the roaring computer business of the 1980s, his company grew six times faster than the industry norm, differentiating itself not by the products it offered but by the way it sold them. Duane founded The Sales Board in 1990 to teach the skills of Action Selling to others.